Poem from the author

I was once a young girl who wanted to grow up to be a doctor, unfortunately my family stood by to ignore it.

Don't get me wrong, my life is okay, but what if they recognized me and who I wanted to be so that I could aspire to my own greatness some day.

There is nothing like a dream that dies as it multiplies and is often covered by flies and gnats all things yucky.

This doesn't have to happen to your child, not when you take that time to make them smile, help them learn to grow-help them to learn all that they can know.

Don't get me wrong, I love my family.

They were the most educated but I was subjugated.

I was relegated by lies they thought were true, but now looking out of the corners of their eyes, "Ungh, she's successful. She's independent."

Give your child all of you and I hope that this book encourages you to pay close attention as your clay (child) is meant to surpass you and you're in charge of molding it.

Don't skip a beat for it will be, you, your child and the world you cheat.

Shana Trahan October 6, 2018   10;44am

Chapter 1

Shortest yet complete parent guide

Many people set out on the journey of parenthood uncertain of what to do and how to do things. Some people think that they want to do things just like their parents while others swear up and down that their parents or guardians are the last people they will pattern themselves after. Some people read books while others take parenting classes and others even talk to their friends whose children are still alive past the age of one. And then there are others who have had a great hand in helping with younger siblings, cousins, nieces, nephews, neighbors or younger children and babies in church. Finally, there are the people who get pregnant, give birth and wing it.

Some of you take Lamaze classes, exercise during pregnancy, read books aloud to your growing baby or even meditate. Others, unknowingly are drinking or using some type of medications, doctor ordered or not at the beginning of the pregnancy before knowing that there is a living, breathing life inside of you. Some people take second jobs to be able to buy more things the bundle of joy will need during their arrival into this big world while others stop working to reduce the stress on themselves and the little person growing on the inside. What separates a good parent from a not to good parent? Should we look at the extremes or consider the mainstream?

How do I see myself and my actions as

related to the topic in Chapter 1?

_____

_____

_____

_____

What have been some interactions experienced

related to the topic in Chapter 1?

_____

_____

_____

_____

What can I do more of or change to become

that great parent I'd like to be?

_____

_____

_____

_____

_____

_____

Chapter 2

The first way to be a good parent

What a good parent was to me changed a bit from my pre-parent years to being an actual parent and having to be fully responsible for the life of another human being. Just the thought of having to be responsible for their 24 hour safety, providing a place to live, food, water, wisdom, education, compassion, thoughtfulness, candor, insightfulness and so much more was incredulous. Choosing a daycare was probably one of those things that most people struggle with, especially when your child can't speak to tell you about their day.

Luckily, my daughter won in this area. There was a daycare not too far from where I grew up that was family owned and run by a mother and daughter. They appeared to be quite genuine and were always thoughtful and considerate. The facility wasn't state of the art, but it was clean, had all of the expected amenities at the time and most of all, it was apparent that the mother/daughter duo loved the kids. That, for me was priceless.

All children are different and my daughter was a kid who played hard. When I was growing up they would have called her a tom boy. She was always sent to school in her very pretty red plaid

top with a white collar and a piping around it and

the cutest little bottoms. Her hair was always

neat and in place. At the end of the day, when I

picked her up-and sometimes my mother, her

face and hands would be clean. She would be dry

and each strand of her cottony soft curly brown

hair would be in its place.

You're probably thinking, what does any of

this have to do with anything. Remember,

When you leave your child at daycare, it's like

leaving them with their second mother. That

person should be nurturing, caring, kind, loving,

thoughtful, helpful and most of all fully interested in the growth and development of your child.

In this day and age, many daycares are just money factories. You have to be able to tell the difference between the facility that was built with your child in mind and one that was just built to take the money in.

Some things to look for:

1. Are the people cold in nature?

2. Can you visit anytime without a call?

3. Do you hear lots of crying all the time when you visit?

4. Does your child fret going back after attending for at least 2 weeks?

5. Is your child returned to you clean with washed hands and a washed face?

6. Is your child dry or prompted to use the restroom before leaving?

7. Does the center smell truly clean?

8. Does it appear safe or are there unusual hazards?

9. Are there enough staff to take care of the children?

10.   Do they have cameras?

11. Are there strange people lurking around who have never been introduced and who don't teach the kids?

12.   Is the Director willing to show you the background checks on ALL staff if asked? (Must be in their employee file)

13.   Do your child appear to be happy at the end of their day?

This is one of the ways to be a good parent. In a professional development I attended yesterday, it was reported that 1 in 10 children will be sexually assaulted by the age of 18. While it often happens by a family member or someone posing as a friend, it's super important to be thoughtful about which strangers you leave your baby, infant, toddler or child with.

How will you research daycares and pre-schools?

_____

_____

_____

_____

What is your budget for childcare?

_____

_____

_____

_____

What are the top three things you require in a child care?

_____

_____

_____

_____

What are the pro's and con's to allowing a family member to take care of your child?_____

_____

_____

_____

_____

Chapter 3

Another way to be a great parent

Give your child what you gave them the first nine months. How much different do you believe humans would be if they spent 9 months between a petri dish and and incubator outside of the womb? Many ponder, from where does a sociopath or a psychopath grow? Whether your child was planned or unplanned, he or she needs your time. Spending meaningful time with your child from birth through age 18 is important.

Having been in education for more than 18 years at every level, except for graduate school it's fair to say that I've seen my fair share of students and parents/guardians. The students who had the most self confidence and performed the best, overall were those who had parents who were present, available and participating in the life of those children. So, some of this is related to planning. Over the years, many parents who chose to have multiple children while earning a meager income ended up working multiple jobs to make ends meet.

The end result is that children end up raising children. The oldest child starts taking on adult responsibilities and in turn attempts to take on an adult persona at school where its not widely appreciated of a middle schooler or accepted. Next, you receive a call from a teacher or administrator about your child's choices. He or she has been set up for failure because your teen isn't a grown up and is expected to be respectful to adults at school. Then you either keep that second job and watch your eldest child's grades suffer because they are too busy making sure the younger siblings are doing their homework, eating and taking a bath.

Children raised by technology are more distorted emotionally and mentally. They are much more disconnected. Tech in limited quantities is fine. There are multiple apps and internal settings by which you can monitor them and set time limits on specific programming. The second way you can be a great parent is by spending time with your child. Your child can sit in the kitchen and do homework while you're cooking or perhaps they can share in cooking with you. Also, you can plan family game night, or pot luck every other week with extended family.

Another great way to spend time with them is

bath time depending on their age. Also, time at

the park, reading bedtime stories to them or

letting them read one to you. You can also go

through their backpack and check their

homework. Make sure it meets standard based

upon their age. Discuss school, friends and

classes. There are millions of ways to develop a

close knit relationship with your children. While

you love and are devoted to your children, it is

healthy to let them sleep in their own bed.

Babies and young children should not be sleeping in the bed with their parents.

Did your parents spend meaningful time with you? If so, what did that look like?

_____

_____

_____

_____

If not, how did that make you feel? How do you think that has affected you as an adult?

_____

_____

_____

_____

_____

_____

Chapter 4

Remember, no matter how much schools

contribute to who your child will become, you are

your child's first teacher. For this single reason,

you will want to look into the mirror to evaluate

yourself. Who are you? Are you your best self?

What can be improved upon? How you you want

your child to see you? What type of role model

do you want them to have in you? Can you be a

role model for your child? Who will they see

when they look at you? What type of future do

you want for your child? Have you achieved that?

What financial goals do you envision for your

child? Do you see that for yourself? If you love

yourself but realize there are a few things you'd

like to change before your child realizes the

current reality:

- List them in order from shortest to longest

  to accomplish.

- Decide how and when you can start on your journey.

- Realize the long term benefit to your child.

- Do what you can to be the best parent you can be.

Our children look at us as superheroes for a long time. They think parents can leap tall mountains in a single bound and cure all ills. The reality is we want to move mountains for them and anything else to make them happy and to see them have a good life. Sharpen your skills. Improve yourself. Think about that one day your child will come home and say, "I can't do that math problem" or "I can't run around the field two times". What will you say? Will you tell them don't worry about it or will you help them to attempt to conquer it? You deserve all that is good. You must be convinced of this because if your confidence is low, your child will know it. Put down this book and think about yourself for a few days. Make your plan. Possibly get an accountability partner, someone who will be positive with you and help you meet your goals by being a support to you.

Top 3 Goals

_____

_____

_____

_____

_____

_____

Goal 1 -Steps to make goal 1 reality

_____

_____

_____

_____

_____

_____

Goal 2 Steps to make goal 2 reality

_____

_____

_____

_____

_____

_____

Goal 3 Steps to make goal 3 reality

_____

_____

_____

_____

_____

_____

_____

_____

_____

_____

Chapter 5

I will do what you do, not just what you say

Whether married or not, your child is observing how you create, maintain or destroy relationships. They listen to your conversations and observe how you value or devalue others. This is most true when considering their mother, father, grandparents and siblings. A good rule for problematic communication is that it should not be in earshot of the children. When children hear parents argue or worse see them become physical, they begin to develop insecurities that takes a much longer time to restore than to destroy.

For many, we repeat what we know, what we've seen. In this current culture, perhaps it's what was on The Housewives of Atlanta or Keeping Up With the Kardashians. There is an overwhelming amount of media enforcing an idea that anything goes. Parents help to form their children's opinions about people, life, experiences, expectations, values and behaviors. If we don't consider our actions or interactions in the faces of our children, we are doing a disservice to them. A way to be a great parent is to consider the communication and interactions you expose your child to. I distinctly remember my mother downing my father over the years.

This was after they divorced. As a child, it

caused my feelings toward her to grow sour. She

never knew why it was so hard for me to get

close to her. That is the main reason over all of

these years why we talk but my relationship was

closer to my father. He never had a bad thing to

say about her. He showed me respect by doing

that. Another example that I'd like to use are my

great grandparents. They were married more

than 75 years. They were so peaceful. They knew

what they meant to each other. They talked

about the things that they were concerned

about-they didn't argue. They showed love,

kindness and respect. Though I wasn't living with

them, we could hear every sneeze my great

grandmother made in my grandparents home

nextdoor. If we could hear her sneeze, we

certainly would have heard arguing and loud

disagreements.

So, you won't just be a standard parent

when you consider and effectively manage your

interactions with others in front of your

children, you'll be a great parent. Others will

want to know, "Why is your child so well

adjusted?". Remember, we are modeling for our

children for their future. While they don't fully become us, the foundation and values will translate into their adult households one way or another. This is up to you. How can you do this? How can you get your partner to agree? Like Nike, "Just Do It!"

What people on earth are in charge of shaping and molding your child?

_____

_____

_____

_____

Have you fallen victim to letting technology raise your child because you've been too busy? If so, what are three things you can do to change that today? Who can hold you accountable?

_____

_____

_____

_____

_____

_____

How do you envision your child being as a grown up? What kind of citizen, friend, husband, wife or parent do you see them being based upon what they have learned from you or your household?

_____

_____

_____

_____

_____

_____

If this is what you want, excellent! If not,

what must you do now to improve the outcome

of your child?

_____

_____

_____

_____

_____

_____

Chapter 6

There is no perfect life. For a young child

it's important to establish for some key things.

They are: stability, safety/security, community,

value in self, values for life, experiential learning,

structure, open communication, belief their

words and love that is unwavering. We teach

these things by everything our children see and

hear us do. If we divorce, walk away from them

because of being upset with the other parent and

don't give them the benefit of our greatness,

that child could ultimately learn something from

you leaving. Perhaps, as in many cases, they will

learn to abandon people and situations. For some situations, it certainly can't be helped (abuse, cheating, drug abuse), but most things can be worked out if the adults involved purpose themselves to learn more, to be committed to the process-even if it involves counseling. For stability, it is important to establish a place to live that won't be disrupted too much.

Safety is important in the home, at church, in the homes of relatives and friends and in the community. According to Increased child abuse, more abuse and unfortunately, even child deaths have occurred. So, it's important to keep your child safe, unfortunately that could be away from your spouse or uncle, sister or cousin, etcetera. This doesn't mean to live your life in absolute fear. It means that you are responsible for teaching your child about the private areas covered by a bathing suit should not be touched by anyone but them. They need to be taught that any touch that makes them feel uncomfortable they can reject and to report it to you. It makes children feel secure when you believe them and they know that you will stand up for them (unless they were cursing in the middle of teacher Mulroney's classroom).

Community is important and can be established within a group, organization or within family. If a child is taking gymnastics, for instance, the gymnasts might spend time together and create events for the children to spend time and develop relationships.

Children feel valuable when they have a purpose. When they can be applauded for doing something well. The feel valuable when they are loved for just being them. Children feel valuable when they are prioritized in the lives of their parents and family. Children feel valuable when we, as parents listen to them.

When my granddaughter was 3, a month ago, she would say, "Nana, I am talking!" Woe! Three years old, valuing her contribution. If anyone else was talking, I'd silence them so that she could share what was important to her. In the long run, priceless. I expect that she will learn from this that she can tell me anything, all things. This can keep her safe.

Some people didn't have a background filled with lots of wonderful and valuable experiences. However, it doesn't mean that your child shouldn't have a wealth of experiences. For each family, that will look different: Boys and Girls

Club, YWCA/YMCA, Tennis, Tumbling, Football, Baseball, Basketball, Rowing, Archery, Soccer, Academic Games, Singing, Acting, Dancing, Traveling, Explorations of the state where you live and more. Many free events and opportunities can be found in most cities and states. Some will be offered through your child's school. If you visited every state or national park in your state, you'd be taking lots of trips, thus experiences. Set a purpose for *each trip.*

Children learn from experiences. Experiences help to shape children into strong and capable adults. After all, isn't this what you want for your child?

Remember, it's quite important to allow your child to express a healthy interest in activities he or she would like to partake in. As parents we certainly would like to ensure they have a certain foundation, however; the child should be encouraged to explore areas they note are of interest to them.

Lastly, as it is quite tempting to make a child choose a career field that you want them to pursue, your relationship could be adversely impaired if they aren't able to decide their own path, their own future. This is their freedom and right. There is almost nothing worse than going to work daily, hating it and needing to go back tomorrow because your family is depending on you.

Have you considered events or activities that you believe your child might enjoy?

_____

_____

_____

_____

Do you plan to force your child to participate in only the events you want them to

participate in or will you allow them some

healthy flexibility and freedom to choose?

_____

_____

_____

_____

What is a fair and healthy way that you and

your child can plan activities that are

worthwhile? Consider asking your child.

_____

_____

_____

_____

_____

_____

_____

_____

_____

Chapter 7

To support or not to support

Children grow through guidance and support

of their parents, family and extended family

such as church, school and other affiliates. To be

a great parent, you'll want to support your

children in their endeavors. Sometimes it might be something you have an irrational fear of, but don't discourage curiosity and creativity. A friend of mine has a fear of flying. She has never flown. In turn, she has created a family of non-fliers by discouraging them based upon her irrational fear. For example, more people are killed in auto accidents than by flying and she drives a car daily. So, now what?

Recently, I've seen more parents helping their children to make dreams come true. I guess one of the first events that made me think about it was Lemonade Day. Parents helped children to learn about money, serving others, how to treat others one fell swoop. Some of those very children will grow up and choose to be entrepreneurs because of an experience like that one. Other parents are supporting children in so many business opportunities that can be seen on Shark Tank and all over the web. Some children choose to do something just because they enjoy it and end up helping others in the process. Life is about connecting and about children being supported well by parents from 0-22 so that they will launch successfully. You can show your support with words and with actions. If your child wants to learn about something that a friend of yours does, ask your friend for some time to show your child some things or answer some questions the child might have. Go to www.Amazon.com , Barnes and Noble or that great independent book shop near your home to research the topic and make choices about what will be done and how you can best support your child.

If your child hasn't come up with any ideas, perhaps you can ask them if they'd like to collect hats for the homeless. Teach them that service is key. Giving is cyclical. Teach them to dream and to strive for the dream.

How can you support your child being a dreamer and a doer?

_____

_____

_____

_____

Did anyone support you in your goals and vision for your future?

_____

_____

_____

_____

How did that support or lack of support feel?

_____

_____

_____

_____

_____

Chapter 8

Give your child the gift that keeps on giving.

You ask, what is that? Hmmm. Well it's something that I wished my mother or father knew enough about to have taught me more. The topic money, valuing it, income, budgeting and savings. In my experience, an extremely rewarding venture with children has been sharing my budget. Some books I read about money came from Robert Kiyosaki, Dave Ramsey and Suze Orman. They were impactful. No, my account hasn't reached millionaire status, but there are some amazing things that came out of our multiple meetings. So, I used the budgeting tool from www.daveramsey.com and his daughter has a different tool on www.everydollar.com .It

depends on you as to which you'd prefer to use.

So, I create a new budget for each month

because sometimes things are paid off and the

payments have to be put somewhere else in the

budget. So, I showed them my paycheck stub and

began to explain the gross, the net, FICA,

retirement deductions and more. They stared in

awe at the difference between my gross and net.

I showed them my bills: mortgage, car note,

electric bill, etcetera. They were all on a

spreadsheet. We discussed percentage of income

being used in each area. They were asking

questions and presented multiple scenarios. It was just a clarifying time watching them very interested and excited to learn something that some households have taught is a grown up thing. When children know your reality they understand if now is a good time for a new outfit or if they might need to choose to wear something they already have.

As a result, my son worked part time while in his senior year of high school and he saved upwards of $5,000 to use towards school, despite 90% of his college being paid for by scholarships. He is attending a tier 1 university and he has no student loans. Teaching children the value of money early can save you and them money in the long run. If you don't happen to know much about it, perhaps access one of the resources that I shared earlier. As parents, we don't have to know everything, just where to find or learn what we want to find or learn.

Did your parents teach you anything about money? _____

What did they teach you?

_____

_____

_____

_____

_____

_____

Do you feel as if your adult life could have been improved if someone had taught you about more than how to earn and spend money?

_____

_____

_____

_____

_____

What things do you think are important for

your children to learn and know about money?

_____

_____

_____

_____

_____

How will learning and knowing those things help

your child to have a better life as an adult?

_____

_____

_____

_____

_____

_____

_____

Do some research, which sites and links can

be useful to your learning and teaching about

budgets and money management?

_____

_____

_____

_____

_____

_____

Chapter 9

The final Chapter

Yes, all of the ways that I have shared with

you about how to be a great parent are relevant,

real, honest, authentic, tried, true and tested.

It's important to teach your children about

money and budgeting. When they are young so that when they are young adults and adults they will respect what and how money should be used. It's extremely important to ensure they feel stable, safe and secure. A secure child will take risks for things that make sense and end up more successful than the young person who becomes an adult and has never taken any risks. It's dire to listen to them and support them. Let your children know that you love them and that you always will.

I had an adult to tell me once that they believed one of their children was gay. They noted how difficult it was for them to accept because of their particular career. I shared, "If this is true, the child is still yours. How could you love the child any less?" Children will often give in to what is natural for them or things they may choose that we do not choose for ourselves. As long as it isn't drugs, prostitution or things that are tremendously harmful to themselves or others, just support and love them and accept their choices. To get them to stay on the same path as you planned for them comes with emotional support.

Giving them your time is priceless because it causes them to value you and your words more than that of their peers. When they are approaching 18 or that time to go off to college, the military, a trade school or to work, trust that they will be working from the foundation that you have set for them. They will learn and grow, experience some new things and meet some new people. Ultimately, if you set that solid foundation, you won't have to worry about them. They will be just fine.

So, this book touches on some points that certainly every new parent should have. Please share this one or buy one for another parent to help them to set a solid foundation for their children. Thanks for reading and applying the wisdom in the text.

References

Some references were made to some wonderful people or their resources. The only person whose signature phrase from a song which was adapted was, "Living your life like it's golden" from none other than the incredible Jill Scott.

www.jillscott.com

Thanks

A sincere thank you to all people and entities

mentioned here in this book. You have positively

influenced me to love how I love, to give how I

give and live how I live.

About the Author

Grew up in Louisiana in a single parent home. Participated in many organizations while in school. Was a devoted member of the U.S. Army Reserves and the U.S. Army National Guard. An officer in the U.S. Army National Guard. A trained Patient Care Technician. Worked in multiple medical settings to include Psychiatric Hospitals. Graduated from Southern University of New Orleans, University of Phoenix and Lamar University. Undergraduate degree is in Psychology. Initial master's in Diverse Learners and the second master's in School Counseling. Served in the education arena for 18 years. Currently, finishing up Licensed Professional Counseling Internship. That should be completed by March of 2019. Employed as a School Counselor.

www.ingramcontent.com/pod-product-compliance
Lightning Source LLC
Chambersburg PA
CBHW060536030426
42337CB00021B/4295